THE CENTRE FOR ENTERPRISE,
We are a think tank based in Oxford that
market economy built on ethical foundati

We undertake research on the interface of Christian theology, economics and business.

Our aim is to argue the case for an economy that generates wealth, employment, innovation and enterprise within a framework of calling, integrity, values and ethical behaviour leading to the transformation of the business enterprise and contributing to the relief of poverty.

We publish a range of material, hold events and conferences, undertake research projects and speak and teach in the areas with which we are concerned.

We are independent and a registered charity entirely dependent upon donations for our work.

Our website is www.theceme.org.

For further information, please contact the Director, Revd Dr Richard Turnbull, at:

The Centre for Enterprise, Markets and Ethics
First Floor, 31 Beaumont Street,
Oxford OX1 2NP

About the Author

Steve Morris is a Church of England parish priest in London. Before that he was a writer and ran a brand agency. Steve has written books about management and organisations. He is married and has two children and three cats.

The Centre for Enterprise, Markets and Ethics

Enterprise and Faith Series

Enterprise and Entrepreneurship:
Doing Good through the Local Church

Steven Morris

Copyright © 2018 Steven Morris

This edition: Copyright © 2018 The Centre for Enterprise, Markets and Ethics

The moral rights of the author have been asserted.

The views expressed are the author's own and do not necessarily represent those of CEME, its board or staff.

All rights reserved. This book or any portion thereof may not be reproduced or used in any manner whatsoever without the express written permission of the publisher except for the use of brief quotations in a book review.

Scripture quotations are from New Revised Standard Version Bible: Anglicized Edition, copyright © 1989, 1995 National Council of the Churches of Christ in the United States of America. Used by permission. All rights reserved.

First edition 2018

ISBN: 978-1-910666-13-5

Published by: The Centre for Enterprise, Markets and Ethics, 31 Beaumont Street, Oxford OX1 2NP

Design by: Push Start Marketing Ltd, 46 Market Square, Witney, Oxfordshire OX28 6AL

Printed in the United Kingdom by Foremost Print Ltd, Unit 9a, Vantage Business Park, Bloxham Road, Banbury, Oxfordshire OX16 9UX

Contents

1.	Enterprise and the Church	7
2.	An Entrepreneurial Vicar	15
3.	Doing Good – The Bread and Butter of the Church	23
4.	Models of Enterprise and Church	33
Conclusions		43
Notes		48

One can tell the story of missionaries who have set out with the firm determination to do nothing except preach the gospel, to be pure evangelists uninvolved in all the business of 'social service'. But the logic of the gospel has always been too strong for them. A hungry man comes asking for food; shall he be refused in the name of the gospel? A sick child is brought for help. There are children all around with no opportunity for schooling. And so the missionary has been drawn, in spite of pure theology, into the work of education, healing, social service ... and a host of similar activities.

> Lesslie Newbigin, *The Open Secret: An Introduction to the Theology of Mission* (London: SPCK, 1978, rev. 1995), p. 91.

Chapter 1
Enterprise and the Church

For me, thinking about enterprise and entrepreneurship is natural. I grew up in a family that ran a business and I worked behind the counter for many years with my mother and father and brother. I learned a great deal about business from my parents. They believed in enterprise – that we should work hard, make the most of our talents, be productive members of society and that we should do good. They never set foot inside a church.

My father's journey took him from the bombed-out slums of the East End of London, via National Service, to being a company director, acquiring his own home and finally running a shop. Perhaps there has never again been a period of such social mobility. My mother's family were entrepreneurs from the start, owning and managing a cab company.

I learned that running a business is tremendously hard work and takes commitment and love. I discovered the importance of understanding customers and never judging them. And a little bit of buttering-up does no harm either. Today that is called customer service. I learned that even in a small business, outside forces and trends can have a huge impact – our shop was eventually put out of business by a huge DIY superstore opening up within walking distance.

Although we did not use the word then, my parents were entrepreneurs. They shared the classic features we see in such people: they were alive to opportunities, took some risks, were highly creative and invested much of themselves in a business that was beautiful – perhaps a strange word to use but it reflects how we felt. Like many entrepreneurs, for us making money was not the only focus.

Being enterprising is not for the faint-hearted, but I wondered then if it does not make the world go around, and I know now that it does. And so why is it that the Church seems so uninterested in the world of commerce, enterprise and the dreams and aspirations of entrepreneurs? Or perhaps it might be fairer to say that the Church has demonstrated a mixed response to entrepreneurship and enterprise. On the one hand there is a suspicion that enterprise and business are somehow fatally aligned with greed. Yet alongside that there are some signs of greater sympathy and an embracing of what the enterprise mindset has to offer. It would be hard to argue with John Spence, a member of the Archbishops' Council of the Church of England and formerly a prominent banker, as he highlights the sheer power of recent entrepreneurial activity as embraced and adopted by the Church itself:

> The Church of England got five million people using its website on the day of the Royal Wedding. We have to take Jesus to where the people are and how they communicate and not just expect them to come and sit in pews on a Sunday.[1]

I have begun to wonder if valuing enterprise may be the last link in the chain of how the Church can be both faithful and relevant, and whether we may be on the cusp of something very exciting. If the Church can bring the hope we have in God alongside an outlook that values enterprise and entrepreneurialism, what doors may open? We might transform the social claims of the gospel and help people to understand the good news that is at the heart of our faith.

Perhaps there is, or could be, a bold link between doing good (the social implications of the gospel), building community and an enterprise mindset. Rather than seeing this impulse to do good in isolation, combining this with entrepreneurship could lead to a new flourishing and sense of community in the places where we live.

Edward Carter, formerly Canon Theologian of Chelmsford Cathedral, makes a bold claim – one that I echo throughout this booklet:

> Enterprise and entrepreneurship are not a set of techniques simply to be applied to the Church's problems. They are not simply a tool. Instead they are part of the bridge that connects God with the world and his people. Enterprise and ingenuity are part of our Christian longing.[2]

To put the matter another way: the attributes of enterprise are part of being a joyous, fully functioning child of God.

John Spence has a very powerful take on just why good entrepreneurialism is intrinsically godly:

> The best entrepreneurs use people's skills to their best effect. They reward people for their labours. They help people to know that they have more skills than they thought they had. They are intrinsically humble, because their focus is on others and developing others ... helping them to achieve. Of course, the worst sort of entrepreneurs just want to grind people and milk them for all the money they can make.[3]

The Church, however, has been cautious about entrepreneurship and entrepreneurs. A collection of essays was published before the 2015 general election, edited by Archbishop John Sentamu: *On Rock or Sand? Firm Foundations for Britain's Future*.[4] The book covered a wide range of issues, from welfare to economy, poverty to young people and the welfare state. But the chapter on the way ahead for the British economy fails to mention entrepreneurs at all.[5]

THE WORLD NEEDS US

A few months ago I was at Farringdon in London – the heart of so many creative industries. As I left the station there were simply thousands of people, young and old, streaming into work. Many would be using their talents in small agencies and start-ups, others in more established businesses. But I was struck by how absent the Church seemed in this place. What have we got to say? How are we to connect with all that is good in this enterprising place? If we accept that the Holy Spirit is already at work in enterprise, how do we join in? How can we affirm what is joyous, exciting and fulfilling in enterprise? I will come back to this conundrum later.

Perhaps the problem comes from a deep dualism. It has often been pointed out that evangelicals have retreated from certain areas and industries that seem hostile and unholy – notably entertainment and the arts. Historically that is only partly true, but perhaps more marked is the wider attitude towards business and enterprise, especially in the UK. There is a squeamishness about making money, or the way money is made. We find it difficult to acknowledge that it is the creating of wealth that allows us to have doctors, nurses and teachers paid for out of the public purse.

There can be a division between what happens in Sunday in church and the rest of the week. In conversation, the Director of the Centre for Enterprise, Markets and Ethics, Revd Dr Richard Turnbull, noted that he had known several business people who became priests but then seemed to be captured by the minutiae of church life and positively failed to make any links to enterprise, almost emphasising the gap. So what is our theology of enterprise? And how might we engage

> **'Can the Church be a place where enterprise and entrepreneurs are encouraged?'**

and re-engage with the thrilling world of business and creativity? I wonder if we can do good *and* do enterprise and commerce?

CHURCH LEADERS AS ENTREPRENEURS

In the Church of England, all candidates for ordination go through a long period of discernment, which finishes with a selection board. When I got the report back on my selection conference for becoming a priest, I remember a number of sniffy comments about my 'business background'. The selectors were not sure an entrepreneur and businessman was of the right kidney for priesthood.

Thankfully I had a very supportive bishop and college principal. But now, thinking about it, I wonder if all those years of running a business, handling change, inventing new things and building people up might not be just as holy as a more traditional route. The Church may be, in some respects, becoming more open-minded about the entrepreneurial mindset, but there remain substantial negativity and important questions about how we encourage entrepreneurial types into church leadership. Can the Church be a place where enterprise and entrepreneurs are encouraged?

Jesus and Enterprise

The Church is interested in doing good – it is one of the things we do and have been doing in this country for some 1,600 years. This booklet looks at doing good and building community, and at one famously entrepreneurial experiment that sadly failed. But there are whispers in the Bible that enterprise is less on the edge of things than we perhaps might imagine.

The life of the Galilean fisherman was tough, dangerous and relentless. I have long wondered why Jesus chose fishermen to follow him. Partly it was their characters – their down-to-earthness may have appealed to him. But also they ran their own little family fishing businesses. The chances are they were not hired hands. They would have been people of enterprise.

And then there is the example of Jesus himself. He would have worked in his family business – perhaps a local building company of some kind. He would have served customers and seen close-up the everyday heroism required to open up a shop or workshop each morning. Perhaps he delivered orders to customers, perhaps he spoke with his earthly father about the difficulties and challenges the business faced day-to-day. One wonders what lessons God among us learned from his work as a boy and young man. I am sure he did not despise the world of work or underestimate the challenges people faced. It seems crucial that Jesus worked in a family business – even though that was the only model available. Indeed, one must assume that this business was a profitable one, because

> '*Jesus' earthly family business made profits.*'

there is no other way for a business to be sustainable. So Jesus' earthly family business made profits. This is problematic for those who believe profits are simply the result of exploitation, but not so for those who maintain that business is essentially supplying the wants and needs of a community and receiving a return for the investment and enterprise.

Family business and enterprise go hand in hand – innovation, pride and care in doing a good job, working in teams, understanding what customers want now and shaping what they may want in the future.

Edward Carter, in his stimulating CEME publication, *God and Enterprise*, makes the bold connection that entrepreneurs actually see the world as Jesus did – not using a top-down control model of leadership but instead embodying hard work and extraordinary efforts even in the face of 'failure', thriving on creativity, taking risks.[6]

Yes, the very best entrepreneurs take risks and don't let failure put them off. There is a connection here with God, who takes almighty risks as well and never lets failure get in the way of things.

Perhaps we need to start with a much more positive attitude to enterprise and entrepreneurialism. We want to see how the Church can do good and build vibrant creative communities, and do so in an enterprising way.

We need to begin by tracing something of the recent history of the Church doing good in order to build community. We can then see where enterprise fits into the mix and if entrepreneurship and enterprise, and the impulse to social welfare, are mutually exclusive.

Chapter 2
An Entrepreneurial Vicar

Without the Church, where would this country be? We are a mainstay in looking after those who are in difficulty. The magnificent response of local churches to the Grenfell Tower disaster just showed how we are at the centre of community life and respond immediately to need.

But there is, perhaps, still a big question about how we should do good in the world as it is.

For me, as a parish priest in urban, multicultural Wembley, the challenges are many. Our own parish is more than 60 per cent Hindu. What's more, we are ultra-suburban. There are no shops or meeting places in our parish.

All churches go through cycles. Our previous cycle focused heavily on Sundays. Attendance at St Cuthbert's was low at the time I took up my post there, and we had somehow lost contact with the people in the streets around us.

Renewing the church was a daunting task. How do we re-imagine parish church in an area such as this? To answer this question I need to go back a step, to my time running businesses and being an entrepreneur. As I look back on a remarkable few years, I realise that God does not waste what we have been. He is the great recycler of all that we are and have done.

The entrepreneur before the vicar

Many of things I learned running my businesses have been central in the re-imagining of the parish church. I need to tell that story – partly to acknowledge a reality that has been, and to see how that reality has fed into our own little miracle here.

Perhaps fancifully, I claim a kinship with the Lord of life in that I too grew up in a family business. I saw what it takes to run a business and that it meant a lot of work. Each day in the shop was followed by trips to the wholesalers and there was not much time off. When we were burgled, within hours my parents were open again for business. When they were sick, they never took time off. Like those followers of Jesus, the fishermen, you cannot stop work if your livelihood depends on it. You get back in the boat as long as you need to.

I realised that our family business – little shop – was a true centre of the community. Everyone who came in was accepted and treated with respect, even if they were a bit odd. People came in to chat and to feel less lonely. The local church has more in common with a good local shop than it imagines. I picture the local shop my parents ran as a great place of fun and joy, cups of tea and much sympathy. It was the place that took all their creativity and used it, and was the centre of the place we lived. Church is like this too. (There is perhaps another book to be written about the relationship between a great church and great family business.)

If you run a local shop you become a local 'celebrity'. Good local businesses know how to innovate. They know what their customers want now and what they might be enticed to want in the future – which, of course, is the core of marketing.

I took much with me from growing up in the shop, and when, at 30, I set up my own thing, I realised that my parents' enterprising ways had rubbed off on me. Put simply, I was way happier running my own thing than working for a corporation or large company. I enjoyed being my own boss, standing or falling on my own hard work and talents, and there being a direct line between my work and creativity and the money I earned. Growing up in an ordinary family gave me a great desire to broaden my horizons. This, in turn, made me more comfortable with taking the odd risk along the way.

'Good local businesses know how to innovate.'

It also helped that I was growing up during the tenure of a Conservative government under Margaret Thatcher. Although at the time I was dead set against her, I now understand that without her liberalising reforms, small businesses like the ones I ran would have been stamped out by restrictive practices and the big-boys' monopolies. My brand agency could operate as a collection of freelancers, using new technology and forming small mobile teams running at low cost – we could compete with the agency giants in their swanky London offices. Never before, or perhaps since, could a business stuck somewhere as unglamorous as Hanwell, west London, be in the company of global superstar agencies on a common footing. There was a coming together of a political revolution and a technological one.

I began my time as an entrepreneur having been made redundant from my job as managing editor at the Open College. It was not a disaster at all. I remained friendly with the college and they became one of my first customers. My father suffered with the great shame of redundancy, but by the time it was my turn, everyone I knew had been made redundant at least once. And with my new, rather primitive Mac, based in my back room and garden (on a good day), I could ply my trade as a writer with virtually no costs and a contacts book full of gold.

It was a chance meeting with someone that led to my first real business. I met the CEO of a start-up brand agency based in Farringdon. I did a small assignment for him and job followed job. As I began to do some simple projects for corporate clients, I made a striking connection between two different worlds, and this led to something new. Enterprise works through connecting ideas and skills and through understanding what is needed. An enterprising approach is always looking for different ways to solve problems.

I had worked as an editor for years – applying and developing house styles. I realised that the big corporates did not invest in the love of language and language style the way the newspapers did. When you read the *Sun* you know it is the *Sun* because it reads like it, sounds like it, has a consistent tone of voice and way of seeing the world. I remember thinking: 'Why doesn't big business invest in language in this way?'

The insight I had was that customers invest in companies they like. They are less interested in the selling messages they hear than in being respected and treated with courtesy. If companies could sound conversational, human and warm then customer loyalty would follow. I learned this in my parents' shop; I applied it in my brand agency.

And so was born an agency that pioneered tone of voice for large organisations. For a number of years our homespun agency was a bit of a sensation. I got to travel the world and we worked with one massive organisation after another.

I never felt squeamish talking about money or making a profit. We were honest, paid our staff handsomely and took great pride in helping our customers and our customers' customers.

I learned a great deal, but there were some tough times. Recessions led to redundancies, which was painful indeed. We had to change direction on occasion and set up smaller sub-businesses to handle challenges from the large conglomerate marketing agencies.

But I do remember the great thrill of working in teams with talented people, solving problems and seeing our work make a difference. Without realising it, I went from being a suburban agitator who wanted to work for a pressure group to being an entrepreneurial businessman. One of the things I learned was that I was no less useful, righteous or ethical working in the private sector than in the public. Indeed, the vast majority of businesses we worked for were similarly orientated towards good, treated people well and acted ethically.

It was as though the scales fell from my eyes: pressure groups, virtue-orientated groups, are perhaps no more ethical than your common or garden bank.

When I became a vicar of this tricky parish – my conversion and ordination is another story – I wondered what on earth we were to do. Without intentionally drawing on my past as an entrepreneur, I now see that we used many of those experiences to help this parish do good, build community and do God.

The entrepreneurial social gospel

In classic marketing terms, we needed to find out who our customers were and identify their issues. We wanted to understand what we were working with, what opportunities there were and what we could learn from what had happened here in the past – good and bad.

We walked the parish, we looked at statistics, we spent time speaking to people we met in the street. Yes, we also prayed – we did a lot of this. But we used our minds and we analysed and thought, and chewed over what we found out. I certainly realise that using terms from business and enterprise may seem a bit confrontational. However, I come back to the problem of dualism. If God is in everything, business is not beyond him and is not only capable of being redeemed, but also in its very structure and existence reflects something of the nature and character of God.

We found out some very interesting things about our parish and our church. Our parish is predominantly lived in by older folk. They tend to live in the large family home after the children have left and perhaps moved away from the area. We are more monochromatic in terms of ethnicity than we imagined – Hindus make up the largest group here.

Anecdotally, we heard about two major problems people were experiencing: loneliness and its evil twin cousin, dementia. These issues were common in all ethnicities. We simply found a tidal wave of loneliness and it began to break our hearts. The best entrepreneurs are as much heart people as head people.

So here we were in a church that had not connected particularly well with our parish, a parish in pain. We were the only public building here. We had virtually no funds for 'mission' but we wanted to make a difference.

It was time for a fresh vision. I am a bit of an iconoclast in such things, and having seen every kind of mission and vision document known to man or woman, can say that they are frequently either:

1. utterly dull;
2. overly grandiose – involving world domination;
3. bland and cautious; or
4. bureaucratic and backside-covering.

Sometimes they miraculously manage to be a combination of all four. For me, though, the best of these documents are simple, with enough nuance to let you flex the idea a bit.

What are we in the business of? I always liked Butlin's strapline: 'Number One for Fun!' We too settled on something very simple, but it also had a great call to action. Our vision was: 'To be a Blessing' – that was it. We liked this vision because it came after much prayer and gave us scope to be the church we felt God was calling us to be.

Using this vision and what we knew about the place in which we are located, we decided to set up the simplest ministry we could. Our aim was to connect with the parish, get people used to coming into our church and to associate it with the God who loves people. If we could not get people to visit us they would simply continue to see us as 'that place nobody goes any more'.

In fact when we started we were known as the place where the gym class met and the horticultural society put on shows. I found this painful. Why would people prefer going to a flower show to coming to church?

We used very simple advertising – mainly flyers. But word of mouth has done much of the work for us. In a way, this is not-for-profit entrepreneurialism and enterprise. Or put another way, it is social enterprise in its true meaning.

But we have managed to fund the project through grants and donations, and it continues to thrive. Indeed, we have learned to be incredibly enterprising in terms of hunting for funding. I am not at all squeamish talking about money, putting in grant applications and asking for help – both financial and in kind.

The Results

So we decided to set up a memory café every Thursday. Our aim was to tackle the issues we found – loneliness and dementia – and to do so with love. We included memory games, but all we really needed to begin with was a kettle. These days we have more than a hundred people coming each week and are seeing cafés setting up on our model.

We have regular teams of volunteers coming to help from larger organisations. They come as part of their social responsibility agenda and add a great deal with their verve and joy. They are, without exception, amazed at what church does and is, and frequently have questions about faith, life and purpose.

> '**I call our café a place of mini-resurrections.**'

Our setting up of the café has led to a renaissance of community here, and it attracts a broad cross section of people from all ethnicities. And, gratifyingly, we have got a stable and larger Sunday congregation, although it would be a stretch to say that the church is in full revival.

The café has become a phenomenon. We have a full choir, exercise sessions and a huge sense of joy. New friendships have been made and people have volunteered to be helpers.

I call our café a place of mini-resurrections. People tell me each week how our social-gospel experiment has given them fresh hope and a sense of life now being worth living. So we hear of personal renewal – and the impact on community has been profound too.

We are told by many folk about how the parish now has a sense of centre and that the old atomised days of our suburb are no more. This is a big claim, but we keep hearing it so we want to claim it as truth. One day on a trip over to the pharmacy, the pharmacist asked me to accompany him to his little consulting room. I wondered what I had done wrong. Instead he said: 'I want to thank you for all you have done for my Hindu community. You didn't need to do it and we are very grateful to you.'

What we know is that our place is full of people, full of expectations of community, fun and joy. I see no reason why this should not be the story of church.

Chapter 3

Doing Good – The Bread and Butter of the Church

It is patently true that the Church has been at the centre of doing good over the centuries, although this has not been without controversy. There has been something of a tension between a model of church that promotes primarily salvation and another that promotes primarily good works. Only a few have reconciled this conundrum.[7]

Salvation and doing good should never be seen as separate aspirations, but it is possible for a ministry to become skewed in favour of one. Indeed, Martin Luther himself had doubts. He wondered out loud if the letter of James, because of its strong emphasis on good works, should ever have been put in the Bible. He famously described James as 'an epistle of straw' because it talked about law and good deeds rather than faith, the keystone of Luther's theology: 'You see that a person is justified by works and not by faith alone' (James 2.24).

But as Mark Woods points out, Luther was more conditional than we may have been led to believe:

> Luther doesn't think the author was an apostle. Instead he 'must have been some good, pious man, who took a few sayings from the disciples of the apostles and thus tossed them off on paper'. The author, he believes, 'wanted to guard against those who relied on faith without works, but was unequal to the task'. Luther says he 'cannot include him among the chief books, though I would not thereby prevent anyone from including or extolling him as he pleases, for there are otherwise many good sayings in him'.[8]

The anxiety – and sometimes the reality – is that a good ministry can come apart if it becomes too absorbed with 'social work' at the expense of saving work. Others argue that in fact there is an inevitable trajectory of social ministries – that by their nature they tend to slip anchor.

It is telling that Jesus himself resists the temptation to disconnect the doing good from the message of salvation. He was under intense pressure to be a healer and an exorcist. Indeed, the healing part of his ministry drew the crowds and made him famous. But he scolded people for insisting on signs and healed only a handful of those who were sick and ill. The drink he offered was the cup of life, and that was hard for many to swallow.

We might argue that his preaching ministry frequently left people mystified and caused many to walk away. But Jesus would not separate his ministries – what would be the point of being restored in physical and mental health if one missed spiritually that the kingdom of God had come near?

Jesus was also not against business or enterprise (although he could surely never have imagined its sophistication today), but he was against greed and injustice. Perhaps here we need to be more nuanced. Great businesses have strong ethics and make the very best of the talents at hand. Jesus would surely have spoken strongly against exploitative behaviour but he would have rejoiced in enterprise that celebrated people's gifts, provided a great sense of purpose, supplied communities with both basic essentials and wider wants and generated the wealth that was paid in taxes to fund teachers, social workers, doctors and nurses. Just by running this kind of enterprise, the wealth and innovation that results is a major way of funding a compassionate society.

> '**Great businesses have strong ethics.**'

We must remember, too, that state-funded welfare is not the only option for doing good and supporting a social infrastructure. There is a long Christian history, both Catholic and Protestant, of doing good through voluntary Christian societies.

But what about pure good-doing? How does the Church interpret its mission? My contention is that there has been a crisis of confidence in the doing-good part of the Church's mission (although there are many good examples of that part out there). To an extent this has been driven by the great and radical difficulty of holding together salvation ministry and social ministry. It seems more straightforward for church to outsource some of its social ministries – including to the state – rather than grapple with the issues. What might be the value in a social outreach, for instance, to elderly Hindu folk when it is time-consuming, costs money and may not lead to a single person coming to church? Why would a small church invest huge love, time and resources into outreach to single lonely older folk with dementia when church growth comes with families and youngsters?

For smaller churches, how can we have the resources and energy to tackle enormous issues like poverty, gangs, knife crime, domestic violence or loneliness? For larger churches, focused on growth, how do we fit in the social aspects of the gospel? Who does it and how?

One of the great examples of the difficulty of holding together doing good and doing God featured an almost Shakespearean hero vicar who rose to huge prominence and media stardom, burned bright and fell from the sky, and eventually did indeed become a social worker. His name was Nicolas Stacey, and the story of his South Bank revolution is both painful and inspiring. It is a crucial turning point and a warning from history.

The ghost of the Revd Nicolas Stacey

In many ways the ghost of Nicolas Stacey haunts the precincts of the social gospel. The collapse of his ministry and his exit into social work seemed to have sounded the death knell for a certain model of social and community activism. They seem to speak of the ultimate failure and futility of divorcing social action from preaching the word. Such high hopes were invested in his radical rethink – at least by Stacey himself – that its failure left a void.

At the dawn of the 1960s the Church had been skewered by John Robinson's book, *Honest to God*. Belief in God himself seemed to be at stake. Many of the certainties were gone and it seemed that the Church itself might be swept aside on a tide of relativism and liberalism. The only option was adaptation to the culture and the world.

Nicolas Stacey became rector of Woolwich, in south-east London, in 1960. He was one of those colourful, renaissance-type Anglicans you don't quite get any more. He was, after all, one of the runners pushing Roger Bannister to his sub-four-minute mile. Before that he had served on a trawler and had become an expert in diagnosing venereal disease among his shipmates.

Woolwich was a blast to the system for the young, public-school-educated Stacey. He was in control of three struggling Church of England churches. The area was in the grip of poverty, social deprivation and a huge housing crisis. And the south-London working classes in the area were giving up on going to church in droves.

Stacey implemented a radical yet creative programme, drawing on his marketing skills and teambuilding attributes. Indeed, he raised the money for the experiment by writing articles for London's own leading newspaper, the *Evening Standard*. He decided to tackle the problems of social inequality at source. He closed one of the churches and put together a team of high-powered men from England's top public schools to bring about the changes he was looking for.

He radically changed the eighteenth-century parish church of St Mary Magdalene. The old furnishings were swept away and replaced with offices and counselling rooms. He set up a disco in the crypt and a thriving youth club. He opened a coffee bar and art gallery. The premises spawned a housing association and hosted the fledgling Samaritans. Within a short while, more than 1,500 people a week were coming into the church.

But there were telling criticisms and concerns. One cleric, looking on this apparent success, commented: 'If Stacey thinks he can build the Kingdom of God by frying eggs on the altar and percolating coffee in the organ pipes he should think again.'[9] It sounds harsh, but in the end it seems Stacey began to agree.

Stacey did so many admirable and perfectly sensible things. He started a vast programme of parish visiting. He was, when all is said and done, a priest. However, perhaps he was hearing voices of concern in his own mind. He and his team wanted to see people saved and in church, but it wasn't happening. He was concerned that just doing good seemed to be a blunt instrument.

These are voices of concern I understand. After four years Stacey had a moment of epiphany. He wrote two articles for *The Observer*, declaring that the Woolwich project had failed. On a Sunday only an extra 50 worshippers were coming and most of those from outside the parish. London's working class had avoided the need for the church – they didn't come along. Loving them in the week didn't seem to link with a sense of God's love as expressed through his Holy Church.

The articles caused a storm. Among Stacey's suggestions were that parish priests should go out and get a paid 'real job' during the week. His bishop was so traumatised by the articles that he never spoke to Stacey again. *The Observer* invited responses from commentators, among them the eminent sociologist Bryan Wilson, who wondered if the second article should have been titled 'How the Church might surrender' rather than 'How the Church could survive'.[10] Three years later, Stacey switched jobs completely and left his role as a priest in the Church of England.

What are we to make of it all? Was Stacey too quick to call his mission and ministry a failure? Was it crass to equate numbers on Sunday with winning or losing? Was he missing a key element?

Perhaps at root was the ethos of 'doing to' the poor and needy rather than 'doing with'. For a good old patrician public schoolboy, being in the driving seat may seem the right option. In his book, *Who Cares*, Stacey admits that he had problems relating to his working-class parishioners, although he empathised with their situation.[11] My cockney forebears would probably have done just what their modern counterparts did: if some posh geezer is putting stuff on a plate, take it and scarper. I think I would have done the same.

Here's the rub: would adding more spiritual content have filled the church with sold-out believers? I am not sure it would. Perhaps the church services on offer were long and boring (even with the welcome changes to the liturgy that Nicolas made). Perhaps it was more fun going to a knees-up at the pub. Perhaps his regular churchgoers were a bit uncomfortable with the great unwashed spoiling their church with their coarse voices and problems coming out of their ears. Perhaps the wily old Londoners just didn't buy the spiritual content on offer. I wonder if a single member of the leadership team had gone to a state school. I wonder if one of them had been unemployed, poor or came from a broken home.

Perhaps the revolution on the South Bank was not revolutionary enough to cast off the very things keeping people in their place and making them rebel against authority (and that included the Church). Despite looking radical it was neither radical enough nor, if that failed, orthodox enough.

I think that my hero, Jimmy Porter, the main protagonist in *Look Back in Anger*, may have seen through the whole wretched business and given it a finger in the air. Or better still, Wolfie Smith and his Tooting Popular Front, of the 1970s television series *Citizen Smith*, might have seen it for what it was – after closing-time of course.

But perhaps this all says more about me than about the Woolwich project and the demise of South Bank religion. It is an act of bad faith to force history through the mincing machine of modern perceptions. The Woolwich project was a microcosm of the attitudes of the day. History will look back on our puny efforts and ask lots of the same questions we ask about those of our forebears. It is easier to see the past's flaws than our own.

Nicolas Stacey and his team *looked* to be radical in the spirit of Jesus' radicalism. They wanted to do good work and had become exasperated by the sense that the Church had only decline to look forward to. They used the skills of the modern marketer. They knew something important: that the Church needed to change and that there were real people out there who were hurting and needed help.

It is the same dilemma faced by a press photographer. Do you take a photo of a disaster or put your camera down and help the victims? I would make a terrible photographer – I would rather help. There is a weakness here. The war photographer who stopped to help might miss the one defining image that would touch hearts and minds and change everything.

Jesus was confronted with the same dilemma. He was surrounded by suffering. It was an age with no medicine, no social services, no benefits and oppression everywhere. And yet he said, 'For you always have the poor with you, but you will not always have me' (Matthew 26.11). He did not heal everyone. He helped only a handful of people. Why? Because he could.

Because he was touched by each individual's plight. But also to show people a little of what God's kingdom was like and who he was.

I am interested in the great dilemma the authors of the Woolwich project faced because I feel that many priests now face the same one. They come into ministry wanting people to be saved and to help tackle the poverty and hardships they see around them. Where can they do the most good? This is especially true when faced with people in real social or economic need.

I wonder if Stacey was torn between the Sunday numbers and the weekday thriving. It would be easy to say that this was just a failure of vision; that if only he could have understood that God was in the bingo and the café and the housing work, he would not have needed to worry about Sunday.

But it isn't as easy as that. I want people to come to church on a Sunday because that is the real deal. That is where we worship and experience the Eucharist and travel together with Jesus. I know in my heart of hearts that bingo, coffee shops and youth clubs cannot and will not be the answer to our long-term destiny and hope. They are bound to run out of steam.

Thinking about it, I do not blame Stacey for calling on his friends to help, even though they may have come from similar backgrounds to his. You call on those at hand; Jesus did the same.

The issue for me is that Stacey perhaps stopped too soon. I certainly understand his disappointment; the sense of hopes dashed; that amazing social action isn't having any impact on people's more orthodox spiritual lives. But how much time do we leave? When do we say enough is enough? Perhaps we have a new string to our bow now. Perhaps embracing a world that understands enterprise, and seeing God in this, presents an opportunity to do good and do God that is most productive.

Jesus actually took his time. He walked everywhere as the Roman chariots hurtled past. He was so late for an appointment with a sick friend that the friend died. God was easily distracted by the need around him. The key may be for us to slow down enough to catch up with God. We may find him meandering in a backwater or stopping to talk to a woman who has no friends or a man who has gone mad and become a scandal and sadness to his family, who hear only his howls and despair.

I just wonder what would have happened had the Woolwich project kept going, say for ten years, with the amazing Stacey at the helm. We shall never know, but we need to avoid the easy answers.

Jesus seemed to square the doing good/doing God thing perfectly. But then he had an advantage: he is God and knows what he is doing. He is not like most of us, stumbling around seeing things through a glass darkly and wondering what to do next. Jesus' own words are very challenging. He criticises the piling up of 'capital'. In one of his parables he reflects on the futility of business expansion that simply results in bigger barns and surplus stock. He asks a rich young man to give his money away. He encourages people to focus on him and to travel light. But Jesus is not against many of the best aspects of the enterprising society: teamwork, creativity, intuition and joy in discovering new things. And Jesus is not against wealth and its creation; but he does challenge its use.

> **'Jesus actually took his time.'**

Stacey may not, in the end, have changed the Church, but his life of service to others speaks deeply of an impulse to be on the front line. He remained a priest all through his amazing life in the secular world and so never gave up on that ministry. We need more Nicolas Staceys today.

What is the difference between our memory café and the Woolwich experiment?

The Woolwich project, or experiment, had a very different leader who set different targets. Would we have kept going if not a single person had come to church as a result? Yes, and we wouldn't have seen the café as a failure.

Indeed, we have come to see our café as a new kind of congregation and new kind of service. We always pray and we always sing a hymn. The prayers always stress that God loves all people and that all are precious in his eyes.

We see that we now have a new Thursday fellowship and we make no bones that this is church, every bit as much as Sunday, and that we are believers in Jesus. This may shock some readers. There is no sermon. We do not celebrate communion. But we do celebrate the Christian year and we feel that our building, with its iconography and atmosphere of prayer, does much of the work for us.

One of the major differences between our social gospel and the Woolwich project is that we do incorporate our faith into our activities. We pray out loud, we announce the church services on Sunday and we discuss our faith with those of other faiths and no faith. They do not find it threatening because we do it so gently. We also trust our actions to speak as loud as our words. We are relaxed about Sundays and we accept that those with strong beliefs and other faiths are loved by God as well (interestingly, we get many gifts and much help from other faith communities, who tell us that they like it that we do not try to hide our faith).

Nicolas Stacey began to lose heart because his Sundays got no better. He began adding more and more enterprising ideas – his parish was alive with initiatives but they were all rather top-down, and the tougher things got the more initiatives he started. As they tumbled, the leader became demoralised and the parish conflicted. It is hard to imagine the sense of betrayal that must have been felt when Stacey went on to become a social worker and stepped away from parish ministry for good. One imagines that the church took a deep breath and wondered: 'Where to next?'

We see our social-gospel calling as part of the great tradition of the Church. But perhaps there is an even more interesting development to be made that might speak into the lives of all those young entrepreneurs going to work in the city or those wondering if they can set up the business they have always dreamed of.

Chapter 4
Models of Enterprise and Church

I return to the streets of Farringdon, my old stomping ground. As I spend time here I remember just how exhilarating it was being in this kind of environment. It was just the opposite of what the eponymous anti-hero in David Nobbs' masterly television series *The Fall and Rise of Reginald Perrin* portrayed. Perrin was a burned-out, disillusioned executive who simply could no longer believe in the world in which he worked – developing plastic toys for packets of cereals. He takes the drastic step of faking his own death and then setting up an anti-business called Grot that becomes a surprise success.

We see growing confidence in social enterprise helmed by the Church. In Chelmsford Cathedral the English for Women project sprang from pure entrepreneurial thinking. A chance – or providential – double-booking in a room led to some church folk coming into contact with a meeting for Afghan refugees. The resulting smiles and friendships led to a wild idea: classes to teach women English. With no mucking around, the group was formed and is now a model of how cathedrals can respond entrepreneurially to social issues. This was no top-down creation, part of a corporate vision; instead, Jesus-like, it sprang from the front line, wildly creative and done in an instant. This was the very antithesis of decision by committee, more like decision following opportunity and prayer – a very good mixture. One is reminded of Paul's advice to the Ephesians: 'Be careful then how you live … making the most of the time, because the days are evil' (Ephesians 5.15–16). This is good advice for any Christian entrepreneur. And although Chelmsford's enterprising activity is well within the remit of the gospel, perhaps it points us to other spheres of influence as well. The spirit of the Chelmsford work is deeply entrepreneurial. It relies on flexibility, reacting quickly to things on the ground, light-touch leadership and creativity – a potent mix.

> **'We see growing confidence in social enterprise helmed by the Church.'**

How can we foster new communities, new opportunities within the very centre of the business world? The answer is: with doing good and being creative with an enterprise heart. It is like two tectonic plates colliding. New landforms result.

There are two areas on which we can build: learning how we can act in an enterprising way (using the skills of the entrepreneurs); and encouraging entrepreneurs and enterprise.

New Routes
Capital Vision 2020

In 2013 the Diocese of London launched its vision for London – Capital Vision 2020. It is built on three key words and ideas:

1. Sharing the gospel with confidence;
2. Being and showing compassion for those in need;
3. Being creative in the way that we do it.

It also has an interesting focus (target group), namely those in the arts and sport.

> We seek to be more confident in speaking and living the Gospel of Jesus Christ, more compassionate in serving communities with the love of God the Father and more creative in reaching new people and places in the power of the Spirit.[12]

The initiative has a number of major themes, but where it is likely to strike a chord with those in Farringdon and beyond is in its claiming of purposeful imagination for the kingdom of God.

Capital Vison explains that it wants the Church to reach out specifically to those in the arts and in sport, which is certainly a start. Its emphasis on creativity is also likely to chime with those who are entrepreneurs. Perhaps it is a shame that this excellent initiative didn't include them in its scope.

What is welcome is the bringing together of two core values: compassion and creativity. The combination of compassion – the raw business of doing good – with the full creative resources that we have is exceptionally powerful. This is a bold statement that being compassionate, doing good and creating community is a creative act as well as a managerial and process one. If we assume that modern folk are looking for authenticity, a chance to make a difference and to use their uniqueness, then Capital Vision is likely to have traction.

> '*The initiative locates compassion within the context of community.*'

Plus there is also the third strand in the rope: confidence in sharing the gospel of good news. It is a thrilling combination and calls on our resources of creativity to present afresh the message of hope, faith and love that is at the core of the Christian faith.

Rather like the Holy Trinity itself, it is important to keep all three strands together. The gospel comes over much better and more convincingly if it is delivered as part of a programme of love and care and basic attitude to life that embraces creativity, liveliness and joy.

Specifically, the initiative locates compassion within the context of community. Capital Vison talks about creating renewed communities of hope, and this speaks deeply into our lives. Christianity grew slowly but steadily over the first centuries, as a communal activity, and offered a hope that the status quo – with all its cruelty and decadence – was not the way things would be for ever. So the precise emphasis on creating new community is strong in an era when people of all ages report alienation and loneliness as depressing facts of life.

Many city centres now have extraordinary life/work hubs. These are places where people can hire a desk, live, work and be with people of like mind and creative bent. They meet one of the great needs – to belong, to work freely and to be creative – though they too can be lonely places despite all the people. I ask later if this is a space that church can inhabit too.

Capital Vision's rallying call to the arts surely treads fresh ground for the Church and fits perfectly with the folk involved in enterprise:

> Art, creativity and culture are some of the most critical and profound spheres of human activity. From dance to journalism to graffiti, almost everything around you has been touched by the creative industries. Creatives can spark a revolution with a single tweet. [...]
>
> Today's Church is flooded with people whose passion and purpose finds expression in the creative industries far wider than the well-known forms of traditional sacred painting and choral music. We are a people whose work in images, sounds, music, poetry, theatre, design, movement, textiles, sculpture and digital media, shape the city and world around us.
>
> So we're asking: what does it look like to be a Christian and an artist in the weekday workplace? What does it look like for churches to engage creatively with artists?
>
> We want to build bridges and forge language to deepen and enrich interaction between Christianity and the Creative Arts. And we want to connect Christians across London who are already immersed in the creative world of this cultural and captivating city.[13]

If we just added entrepreneurs into the mix this would be a huge step forward. There is another rather obvious issue here: those involved in the arts and sports are a relatively small segment of the population. Enlarging the vison to include work, enterprise and entrepreneurs would have a great deal more reach. It's just a thought.

But Capital Vision is just that: a real *vision* that takes us into some very invigorating waters. It is a neat idea because the three attributes – creative, confident and compassionate – need to be kept in balance.

Resurgo Trust

Also creating waves is the Resurgo Trust. The Trust started in London, at a church in Hammersmith. It is staffed by local residents and aims to transform communities. Interestingly, this particular church probably has a fair number of business consultants, creatives and entrepreneurs in its congregation, but using these resources, it looks both to help young people into work and nurture business starts-ups. The social gospel and enterprise are mutually reinforced.

Resurgo runs Spear, a six-week employment training programme, complemented by a recruitment service for young people. It aims to promote social change by preparing both the employers as well as the youngsters themselves. Then there is the Ventures part of the organisation, which works with early-stage entrepreneurs and helps them with a bespoke six-month tailored consultancy with a team of sector specialists.

These initiatives give great hope that the world of enterprise and entrepreneurship can be embraced by church and that church can be a creative hub in these fields. Questions do arise. You may say that it is easy for an organisation in the heart of London, packed with venture capitalists and business consultants, to do this kind of thing. But that would be hard-hearted indeed. There can be no good reason why any church cannot do something to value people who work or want to set up a venture. Just about any church will have someone connected with it who has run some kind of business and could offer help and advice. Churches often have office space that could be made available to start-ups and fresh new social entrepreneurial activities.

We might call up the government of Margaret Thatcher as a high-water mark of enterprise. The positive legacy of that government continues. The other great opening-up of opportunity in recent decades has been the growth of the internet. Church is beginning to see the huge scope offered by this great revolution. To point out just one interesting entrepreneurial thing that has caught the imagination, let me draw attention to the Bible in One Year app – beautiful and simple, delivering Bible readings and commentary to your device.

Recovering the entrepreneurial

Let us pause for breath. How can the Church prepare the soil for a more open embracing of enterprise and entrepreneurialism? Here are some possibilities:

Pray in church openly and regularly for people in their working lives – Monday to Friday. Make it clear that work is just as holy as church and that God is interested in people at work every bit as much as he is interested in them at church. Pray for entrepreneurs as well as nurses and teachers. Be thankful for work and for colleagues, and for creativity at work.

Reclaim the language of enterprise and entrepreneurialism – neither are dirty words or activities. Capital Vision shows how we can write about work and creative activities with precision and joy. If we can reclaim Monday to Friday we are more likely to win the right to speak into people's lives. But the word 'entrepreneur' does have baggage. Bill Bolton, in his booklet *The Entrepreneur and the Church*, points out that: 'we search for less loaded terms. Perhaps the most popular word at the moment is "pioneer". Other words like "planter", "catalyst" and "builder" have been used.'[14] But these more neutral words don't capture the full measure of what an entrepreneur does, so let's reclaim the word in all its wild glory. Richard Higginson and Kina Robertshaw set out to interview Christians who were also entrepreneurs. They discovered, to say the least, a rather mixed picture of the churches' understanding and acceptance of entrepreneurship. They asked 30 people involved in Christian ministry to comment on the word 'entrepreneur': 'Many respondents were positive ... several responded strongly against it or were decidedly ambivalent.'[15] A flavour of the comments is: 'I loathe the use of the word "entrepreneur". We do not need to borrow terms from the market.'[16]

We have to ask why mere mention of the 'e' word generates such heat. It is troubling. My experiences of being an entrepreneur are both positive and have not harmed my ministry in any way. Indeed, I look back on my time in the world of enterprise as being great fun, great joy and a time in which we paid people handsomely, did great work and learned loads of new things. Money wasn't the main point of it.

Think about how the Church measures success – there is broad agreement that the success of the Church shouldn't just be measured by how many come to church services. John Spence has a strong view on this:

> The Church must get away from seeing success as simply Sunday numbers. Average Sunday attendance is going to go down; people are dying. It will take time to build this up. Instead we should be looking at weekly footfall, the size of the worshipping community and the reach the church has into communities.[17]

Release entrepreneurs within the Church – perhaps we might call these folk 'intrapreneurs'. It is very easy to make change so hard within church that people stop bothering to ask. So are there areas within which we can encourage entrepreneurialism?

Seek out entrepreneurs for the ministry – not everyone can be or wants to be an entrepreneur. Bill Bolton draws a stark picture of those who have ruined their lives in the quest to be an entrepreneur. The Church would be a disaster if it only had entrepreneurs as ministers. But perhaps it could make a little more room for those with an entrepreneurial edge.

Understand – that enterprise and entrepreneurship, and doing good, are not either/or. They can comfortably support each other. In fact a good dose of enterprise thinking in with social outreach can help the latter thrive and vice versa.

Entrepreneurs sometimes fail – but failure is a rich learning experience for them. Indeed, most entrepreneurs worth their salt have clocked up a failure. Odd as this may sound, we could encourage a little more failure – safe failure, good failure. If we try new things and take a risk, some won't work and that's not the end of the world.

Know when to stop – the UK youth movement Soul Survivor took the hugely bold step to stop running their summer festivals. Their statement said that they felt God saying it was time for others to take up the mantle. This is refreshing and just the kind of thing needed to allow new enterprise to come through. Sometimes we need to clear the decks for new people, and/or stop something old so we can start something new. The Bible is full of examples where ministries and initiatives need to stop and fresh starts are required. Sometimes the Church stands by comfortable ministries that have lost their power and freshness.

We should start quickly – strong enterprise is often reactive and swift. A gap is spotted or a need, and the only way is simply to start. We took our memory café from wild idea to opening our doors in three weeks. Church can sometimes seem like the worthy Ents in *The Lord of the Rings* – taking an age to make up their minds as the war comes to their doorstep. Like many large organisations, the Church has processes and committees and a culture of long discernment. In themselves these are not bad at all – but is there a mechanism for quick projects that don't require a great deal of top-down managing? Even individual churches can learn much from the impulse simply to get going, to start.

WHAT DO WE DO WITH OUR WEALTH?

Wealth can be a touchy subject and the Church is notoriously squeamish about it. But what have we to say to people of the enterprise culture who have made money and want to invest it? Gavin Francis set up Worthstone, a place where those looking to invest can do so and also make a social impact. His insights are interesting and perhaps speak to us more generally about what to do about wealth. Gavin realises that: 'People are looking for more than a financial return. If we can show them that their wealth can have a broader impact then they listen.'[18] Many churches hold funds, and of course as good stewards we must be very careful and straightforward with them. But how might we invest the money we hold if we could do so in a project like the following?

> We encouraged investors to put their wealth into a property development LLP in Bristol. The difference was that 80% of those working on the site were ex-offenders. Whereas 25% of offenders serving short sentences are back in prison inside 2 years, in this case the rate was 1%. Our investors saw their investment underpinned by the property and they got a return of 4%. This kind of project could help the church to raise its expectations about what is possible and to open new horizons for our wealth.[19]

Chapter 5

Conclusions

Thinking about doing good, the Church, and building community poses some interesting questions and answers.

THE WHO

The Bible is full of calls to help the needy. Jesus claims that his ministry is to liberate those who are broken hearted and to set the prisoners free. So it isn't surprising that the churches' social action has largely been aimed at those in profound need – and this is quite right of course. Being faced with people in immediate need in our communities drives us into action.

Many will be familiar with Tim Hughes' beautiful worship song, 'God of Justice'.[20] In it he reminds us that God came to rescue the weak and poor. It is one of very few modern worship songs that directly tackle the Church as an agent of social change. Its rallying cry is that we should stop only focusing on singing and should 'go' and do good.

Hughes' song makes a bold statement that the Church and doing good are at the heart of the faith. It is also gentle admonishment to any idea of hunting holy moments at the expense of living out the faith in all the messiness and difficulty of the need we see around us. It seems that the evangelical church is boldly claiming its roots in the social gospel, and hearing a packed hall sing this song – and mean it – is truly an inspiring thing. There are so many amazing examples of the Church answering Hughes' rallying call – with regard to prison ministry, debt counselling, work with refugees and sex workers. Some of these are high profile but there are countless other examples of churches dealing simply with local need in an unfussy and effective way – providing meals, after-school clubs, toddlers' groups and the like. At the beginning of Chapter 2, I asked where this country would

> **'Perhaps enterprise is more godly than we suspected.'**

be without the Church. And I would add to that: where are the countless projects for good set up by Richard Dawkins and his militant-minded atheists? Surely these are good questions.

The Church has a magnificent heart for the lost, and a quest for justice is part of the Christian journey itself. Our own social ministry here at St Cuthbert's, North Wembley, has centred on the lonely and those who have dementia. We started where we saw a need and did the simplest, quickest thing we could to begin tackling the problem.

We had no idea that within a year or so we would be full of people, numbers would be up on Sundays and we would be creating a new community of love and care. We have the sense that God has pushed open doors for us – the Great Entrepreneur has made things happen here.

Capital Vision 2020 takes the Church into the areas of the arts and sport as a fundamental part of mission and connection. The work of the Resurgo Trust broadens the envelope of who we are to do good to – or more profoundly, with. As we extend our definition of what being in need looks like, we open ourselves to new connections and new ways of doing things.

THE HOW (PART ONE)

How do we apply and live our mission to do good? Many will say, quite rightly, that we do good by kindness and care for those in need. In some senses this is all the Church needs and what it has in abundance. God has showered his grace on us and his Holy Spirit leads us into mission.

But this booklet has argued to open up an intriguing new combination. Rather than seeing enterprise and entrepreneurs as part of the great force of mammon, perhaps enterprise is more godly than we suspected and can team up well with the impulse to pour our hearts out to those in need.

Enterprise and gospel are part of living life to the full, following God and blessing the communities we live in and serve. Indeed, they are the glue that creates new communities of care and of creativity and enterprise. This may take some getting used to, but we must acknowledge it as a possibility.

The how (part two)

Nicolas Stacey's doomed experiment in social gospel may have shaken the Church. Even for those who have never heard of him and his project, it perhaps left a legacy of uncertainty about how to do good. It could be argued that we live in a period in which much of the great work churches do is run by para-church organisations like Christians Against Poverty.

The bottom-up leadership and innovation in Chelmsford's English for Women project points to a new model. Stacey perhaps failed through a combination of impatience and a patrician top-down approach. Doing good was something done to and on behalf of the disadvantaged. Perhaps if we take on one of the fundamentals of entrepreneurship, our activities may be less top-down, more spontaneous and more organic in feel.

Arguably, we need to ditch doing good *to*, and see our work on social welfare as a partnership – acknowledging what each party brings. Going back to my image of those streaming from Farringdon Station, this approach of working with groups and listening to them may be a way of opening doors and breaking down prejudices against the Church. Modern folk, who have never set foot in a church and only read some of the narrow and twisted prejudices in the press, are amazed to find a Church that is outward looking, understands their world and challenges, and has much to say and offer in the way of helping others.

Some may turn their nose up at the idea of church searching for relevance, but that relevance is infused with the ancient truths.

Where do we do good?

We are perhaps beginning to look into new hinterlands. As we see the Church reach into the arts and sport and the world of work, we broaden our catchment. We begin to speak about helping to create healthy cities and communities.

Opening our horizons doesn't mean we lose focus on those traditional areas of doing good or the huge social issues with which the Church is beautifully placed to be involved.

But creating new communities where the transforming message, hope and action of Jesus is present is exciting. The danger of course – and I'm sure you spotted it – is that we migrate into 'exciting' areas because these are much less messy than working with people who have addictions, are homeless or suffer from dementia.

In some way, if you feel drawn to the excitement of ministering to a bunch of funky artists or middle-class start-ups, perhaps you might want to put that on hold and set up and run a soup kitchen for a few years first. But perhaps that's just me being an old misery!

AND WHAT ABOUT THE FUTURE?

Could churches be at the forefront of encouraging enterprise – encouraging start-up businesses that help to create a better community? We have many of the things the person currently commuting up to Farringdon Station might want.

We have office space, we have vicars who are around to mentor and encourage, we can offer a kettle and kindness and perhaps the use of a photocopier.

Go to many cities in the UK and you will find start-up hubs and communities. They provide a desk, some companionship, flexible terms and a meeting space. This may feel like a risk for church but nurturing some tender young and worthwhile businesses could be a way of changing lives, building community and connecting with a whole new set of people.

Notes

1. Interview with the author.
2. Interview with the author.
3. Interview with the author.
4. John Sentamu, *On Rock or Sand? Firm Foundations for Britain's Future* (London: SPCK, 2015).
5. Richard Higginson and Kina Robertshaw, *A Voice to Be Heard: Christian Entrepreneurs Living Out Their Faith* (London: Inter-Varsity Press, 2017), p. 37.
6. Edward Carter, *God and Enterprise* (Oxford: Centre for Enterprise, Markets and Ethics, 2016), p. 41.
7. Richard Turnbull, *Shaftesbury: The Great Reformer* (Oxford: Lion Hudson, 2010). See also Church of England (Research and Statistics unit), *Statistics for Mission 2017: Social Action* (London: Research and Statistics, 2018).
8. See https://www.christiantoday.com/article/should-james-be-in-the-bible-martin-luther-didnt-think-so/83458.htm.
9. Quoted in Mark Chapman, 'Theology in the Public Arena: The Case of South Bank Religion', in Jane Garnett et al. (eds), *Redefining Christian Britain: Post-1945 Perspectives* (London: SCM Press, 2007), p. 93.
10. Quoted in Justin Lewis-Anthony, *If you Meet George Herbert on the Road, Kill Him: Radically Re-Thinking Priestly Ministry* (London: Mowbray/Continuum, 2009), p. 39.
11. Nicolas Stacey, *Who Cares* (London: Blond, 1971).
12. See Capital Vision website, https://www.london.anglican.org/mission/capital-vision-2020.
13. See Capital Vision website, https://www.london.anglican.org/mission/capital-vision-2020/engage-more-closely-the-creative-arts.
14. Bill Bolton, *The Entrepreneur and the Church* (Cambridge: Grove Books, 2006), p. 12.

15. Higginson and Robertshaw, *A Voice to Be Heard*, p. 28.

16. Higginson and Robertshaw, *A Voice to Be Heard*, p. 38.

17. Interview with the author.

18. Interview with the author.

19. Interview with the author.

20. The full lyrics may be found online.